NEWMAN'S OXFORD

The Places and Buildings associated with
Blessed John Henry Newman
During his years in Oxford
1816 – 1846

by

Fr Jerome Bertram, MA, FSA
of the Oratory

Composite sketch done to celebrate Newman's return to Oxford in 1880, showing him as a young man in the pulpit of St Mary's, and as a Cardinal in that of St Aloysius, surrounded by buildings associated with his life. *Bodleian Library, MS G.A. Oxon, a.38, fo. 19v, b.*

ISBN 978 1 907380 07 5

Published by

Denis … rd Lane,
K … RP
w … .uk

The Campaign Office
Oxford Oratory
25 Woodstock Road
Oxford OX2 6HA
01865-315816

Printed by
Impress Print, Corby, Northants.

Foreword to the 2010 Edition

The story of Newman enters a new phase with his beatification in September 2010 by His Holiness Pope Benedict XVI. Henceforth 'Newman' is no longer an historical character, the subject of an infinite number of research projects, the quarry for widely differing opinions on religious topics of all kinds – no, now he is 'Blessed John Henry', the subject of a local devotion, the prospective patron of new chapels and churches. No longer restricted to the mind for nominal devotion, now he can reside in the heart, for a devotion that is real.

This new edition is a revision of the booklet *The Oxford of Newman*, printed for the Friends of Cardinal Newman in 1995. Several new engravings have been located and the text amplified in places, but it is substantially the same work. (It is quite different from the booklet, *Newman's Oxford* by Fr Humphrey Crookenden, published in 1966.) We have tried to illustrate it with views taken precisely at the time that Newman was living in Oxford, which was, fortunately, the great age of popular engraving on steel. Many of the steel engravings and woodcuts were prepared for the massive three-volume *Memorials of Oxford* by James Ingram, with engravings by John le Keux after drawings by F. Mackenzie, and cuts mostly by Orlando Jewitt after drawings by various artists. These volumes appeared in 1837, while Newman was at the height of his popularity; while complete copies are now rare, detached engravings and cuts can still be found easily in the High Street print shops. Other contemporary prints have been found to supplement Ingram, while local and national resources have been able to fill gaps. A splendid range of these prints and photographs is displayed in the library of Newman's 'College' at Littlemore, in the care of the Sisters of the Work, to whom we are grateful for assistance.

NEWMAN'S OXFORD

It was only by the merest chance – or may we call it Providence? – that we are not here talking about "Newman's Cambridge". When Mr Newman of Ealing determined to send his son John Henry to a University he had no idea which, "even when the post chaise was at the door, his father was in doubt whether to direct the post boy to make for Hounslow [in the direction of Oxford] or for the first stage on the road to Cambridge. He seems to have been decided in favour of Oxford by the Revd John Mullens, curate of St James' Piccadilly, a man of ability and learning, who had for some years taken an interest in the boy's education. When they got to Oxford, Mr Mullens at first hoped to find a vacancy for him at his own college, Exeter: but failing in this, he took the advice of his Exeter friends to introduce him to Dr Lee, President of Trinity, by whom Newman was matriculated as a commoner of that Society. On his return to Ealing, to inform his school-master of the issue of his expedition, his timid mention of a college of which he himself had never heard before, was met by Dr Nicholas's reassuring reply, 'Trinity? a most gentlemanlike college; I am much pleased to hear it.'"[1] The date was 14 December 1816, and the boy was not yet sixteen years old. Partly because of his youth, and partly because no room was available, he had to wait until the following 8 June before coming into residence in his "freshman's rooms in Trinity".

TRINITY COLLEGE

Trinity College (number **1** on centrefold plan; illustrated inside the front cover and Figs. 1-3) was one of two new foundations made in the reign of Queen Mary in order to train Catholic priests for the reconciliation of England and the Holy See. The pious founder, Sir Thomas Pope, who rests in an alabaster tomb curiously concealed in a cupboard in the college chapel, must be more than pleased with the fruits of his foundation, for his college, as well as providing three martyrs in the sixteenth century, was to educate Monsignor Ronald Knox as well as our own Cardinal Newman.

The oldest buildings of the college, seen on the left in Fig. 1, were originally part of a small Benedictine house, Durham College, founded for monks from the North of England to study at the University. To these was added in 1618-20 the **Dining Hall**, the focus of collegiate life (Fig. 2). Here the portraits of the Founder and the tragic Queen Mary hang on the wall opposite one of Newman by Ouless. Newman's first experiences of

Fig. 1 *The Durham Quadrangle of Trinity College, with the original buildings on the left, the chapel ahead, and the hall on the right; engraving by G. Hollis, c. 1820.*

this Hall were cheerful enough – "At dinner I was much entertained with the novelty of the thing. Fish, flesh and fowl, beautiful salmon, haunches of mutton, lamb etc and fine, very fine (to my taste) small beer, served up on old pewter plates, and mis-shapen earthenware jugs. Tell Mama there are gooseberry, raspberry, and apricot pies . . . Tell Harriett I have seen the fat cook."[2] However, the shy freshman, arriving at a time when most men were going down, soon found things less encouraging. "I am the head of the table at dinner, because I am the only one; at least I sometimes nearly finish my dinner before the few remaining ones drop in. The other

THE HALL; &c.

Fig. 2 *The Dining Hall of Trinity College, seen from the quadrangle. Woodcut by O. Jewitt, for Ingram's Memorials.*

day I had a nice dinner set before me of veal cutlets and peas, so much to myself that I could hear the noise I made in chewing through the empty hall; till at length one came in, and sat opposite to me, but I had not been introduced to him, and he could not speak to me. Consequently we preserved an amicable silence, and conversed with our teeth."[3]

Sixty-one years later Newman was to return to that same Hall as the guest of honour, when he was elected the college's first Honorary Fellow. "In response to the toast of his health he made a speech of perhaps ten minutes in length or a little more in a delightfully simple, natural and generous vein . . . I remember the exquisite finish of his expressions and the beautiful clearness of his articulation and the sweetness of his voice. In particular he referred to one occasion when he went to call upon one of the former tutors. . . . That was Mr Thomas Short . . . he entertained us by conveying indirectly and by a sort of reference that he found Mr Short was lunching off lamb chops. . . . There was something tenderly pathetic to us younger people in seeing the old man come again, after so many eventful years, to the hall where he had been wont to sit as a youth."[4] Among the portraits in the Hall, on the right of the fireplace, hangs that same Thomas Short. He was introduced to Newman as a strict tutor, became his friend and adviser, and in 1878 was still able to welcome his old pupil back to the college, though too frail to join him for that ceremonial dinner. Another portrait, to the left of the fireplace, is of Isaac Williams, who was to be Newman's curate at St Mary's twenty years later. It is remarkable that the archway which leads from the Hall passage towards the kitchen has carved on either side

Fig. 3 *The Garden Quadrangle of Trinity College: Newman's rooms were on the first floor of the building in the centre. Engraving by F. Mackenzie, for Ingram's Memorials.*

of it a heart, just like the hearts on the coat of arms Newman adopted as a Cardinal.

For that first term, Newman moved into a set of "borrowed rooms", from which he tells us that he could see "much snapdragon on the wall . . . the emblem of my perpetual residence even to death in my University."[5] The snapdragon features in some rather poor verses written in 1827, with that same theme of perpetuity:

> I am rooted in the wall
> Of buttress'd tower or ancient hall; . . .
> May it be! then well might I
> In College cloister live and die.[6]

These rooms were at the north-west corner of the college, and had a view west and north towards a high wall separating Trinity from Balliol and St John's. The following term he moved into the rooms immediately adjoining, with the same view (now staircase 14, room 9).[7] After he became a scholar, that is from Michaelmas 1818 to Trinity Term 1821, Newman acquired a most desirable set of rooms in the Garden Quadrangle (now staircase 13, room 4), of which the sitting room looked out over the gardens, while the bedroom had the same view of the snapdragon-encrusted wall. The building, of Wren's design, was erected in 1682 to link the slightly earlier north range to the old quadrangle (Fig. 3). The gardens stretch down to Parks Road, still watched by Newman, for his bust stands at the east end of the north range.

Newman described his sitting room in detail in a letter to his sister Jemima: "On reaching the outer door by the ascent of an elegant flight of stairs the stranger discovers an handsome mat to rub the shoes on, he knocks at the door which is opened by a gentleman of very prepossessing appearance immediately. Who shall describe his amazement! – The room is lofty, and lighted by two windows, from which are seen, the gardens of the college and the turrets of Wadham. Scarlet Morine curtains shed a rich glow over the apartment – Between the windows, half shadowed amid the rich drapery hanging from the cornices, is seen the celebrated Venus of Canova, her hair tied and trussed in the Grecian fashion, and her look averted from the entrance. – On turning to the right a massy chimney-piece of marble discovers itself surmounted by a handsome pair of bronze figures (holding nozzles brilliant with cut glass) and by the soft splendour of a vitreous reflection framed in bronze and gold. Above smiles forth the goddess of youth feeding the eagle of her father Jupiter with the viands of immortality – Still further in the recesses of the room and opposite the windows gleams a circular mirror surmounted by a ball-supporting eagle. – Now turn the view to the fourth side and view in the middle a light grecian vase with sculptured basso-relievos – Upon it stands with unearthly tread the far-famed shooter of the arrow, the Belvidere Apollo – Supporters on each side of the Grecian Deity are beheld the graceful form of the Antinous and the jovial contortions of the dancing Faun. On each side these again, smile the pictures of Reubens and his wife painted by the artist himself and under them two small views of Geneva presented to the owner of the rooms by the Reverend the Dean of the College."[8]

When Newman came back to Trinity in 1878 as an Honorary Fellow, they took him to see the rooms he had occupied in his first year. The undergraduate in residence was Douglas Sladen; he was much embarrassed that the Cardinal saw his photographs of fashionable actresses, but the Cardinal no doubt remembered his own engravings of the Venus of Canova and the Goddess of Youth, and said nothing. After that visit, Sladen wrote an account of Newman's visit and hid it in a biscuit box under the floor, where it was found in 2007, to confirm the identity of the rooms as, indeed, those which the young Newman had occupied nearly two hundred years before.

The pagan Regency splendour of these rooms reminds us that Queen Victoria had not yet been born, and we must envisage Newman's contemporaries as Regency bucks, not sober Victorians. They dressed in bright colours, and wore thin silk stockings and buckled shoes, under the voluminous academic gown. Newman tells us clearly what sort of men most of his fellow undergraduates were like: "Hollis the other day asked me to take a glass of wine with two or three others of the college, and they drank and drank all the time I was there . . . I really think, if anyone should ask me what qualifications were necessary for Trinity College, I should say there was only one, – Drink, drink, drink."[9] He cannot have been really unpopular, for he was frequently invited to such wine parties and asked to bring his violin, though greeted with a roar of applause as "Mr Newman and his fiddle", and plied with the wine bottle from which he "took his time in drinking". Even though one rowdy fellow threatened to knock him down, he called the next day to apologise, and Newman's ultimate verdict on the college was "Trinity had never been unkind to me."[10] The first of his great friendships was formed in his very first week in college, with John William Bowden, who was to remain faithful until his early death, and whose widow and sons were to follow Newman into the Church.

Of all the buildings of the college it was the **Chapel** which Newman most loved, though it hardly features in his correspondence (inside back cover). It was completely rebuilt in 1691, and remains a superb example of an English baroque interior, with exquisite carved wooden fittings which remind us irresistibly of the work of Grinling Gibbons. The ceiling painting of the Ascension by Pierre Berchet was done at a time when any use of representational art in worship was frowned upon, and shows the independence of thought that marked Oxford even in the dark years after 1688. The only alteration to the chapel since Newman's time was the insertion of the stained glass in 1885; the windows were originally filled with small panes of clear glass. To the end of his life Newman was to keep a photograph of the chapel interior in his room. He noted in November 1877, "I look at that communion table, and recollect with what feelings I went up to it in November 1817 for my first communion – how I was in mourning for the Princess Charlotte, and had black silk gloves – and the glove would not come off when I had to receive the Bread, and I had to tear it off and spoil it in my flurry . . ."[11] Communion was a rare ceremony, perhaps only once or twice a year, but all were expected to attend chapel every morning and twice on Sundays, so that for many hours of his youth Newman must have sat or knelt in those sombre stalls or looked up at that daring Ascension.

Newman and his close friends were known as diligent students in a University where most were contented to hunt, to shoot and to entertain, but we must not imagine him as perpetually bent over old books in a darkened library. For a start, he and John Bowden used to go swimming regularly in the old swimming pool at Holywell, naturally unheated (Fig. 4). They also sailed, rode and walked energetically around the city. They wrote and published a long epic poem on the Massacre of St Bartholomew's Day, and in their spare time they attended lectures in the exciting new sciences of geology and chemistry.

Newman was to live in Trinity College from 1817 to the summer of 1821. On 5th December 1820 he took his B.A. degree, though he had only narrowly scraped through the exams, overworking to the verge of breakdown. He still held a scholarship entitling him to rooms in college until the following summer and continued to study, continuing to follow a wider range of scientific interests than were relevant to his degree. At the old University Museum (now the Museum of the History of Science),

Fig. 4 *The swimming baths at Holywell, with Magdalen tower in the distance; lithograph by H. Noison, c. 1820.*

Fig. 5 *Seale's Coffee House, Newman's lodgings at the corner of Broad Street and Holywell; drawing by J. Buckler, 1823. Bodleian Library, MS Don. a.3, fo.74.*

Professor Buckland was demonstrating that the rocks had been formed millions of years before Christ, and showed fossils of strange lizard-like creatures that wandered the earth long before the Flood. Neither Newman nor anyone else at the time thought this was in any way a threat to religion, but simply an unfolding of the wonders of the process of creation. Years later, Newman was quite unable to see what the fuss was about when Darwin published his celebrated theory: he had known and considered it fifty years earlier. "Mr Darwin's theory", he wrote, "need not be atheistical . . . it may simply be suggesting a larger idea of Divine Prescience and Skill."[12] In mid-June 1821 he had to vacate his beloved college rooms, and lodged briefly "at a house opposite Balliol" (**2a** on plan),[13] until 5 July when he rejoined his family in London. He had already reserved rooms for himself and his brother Frank at Seale's Coffee House, where his dear friend Bowden had lodged previously. Here they arrived on 5th October: Newman's plan was to take a few pupils to make ends meet and continue to study on his own. Frank was to be one of these pupils. Seale's **(2b)**

Fig. 6 *The interior of Oriel College Hall, photograph by Henry Taunt, c. 1875. © Images and Voices, Oxfordshire County Council.*

was quite an imposing building of the early eighteenth century (Fig. 5), probably by William Townesend, "the leading Oxford master-mason of his day".[14] It stood at the east end of Broad Street, and survived until 1883 when it was replaced by the Indian Institute. As a place to lodge "it is handy, as having dinner etc. all under one roof."[15]

Here then it was that Newman conceived the ambitious idea of standing for a fellowship at Oriel College, one of the most prestigious academic posts then available. The examination was held in Oriel, and lasted for three days of written papers, in the dining hall (Fig. 6), where they were "supplied with sandwiches, fruit, cakes, jellies, and wine – a blazing fire, and plenty of time."[16] Curiously the first day was Holy Saturday, not then considered as in any way a holiday. Newman reports he was "possessed with the idea that I had all but disgraced myself, and stiff, oh how stiff! with sitting 8 hours on hard benches, I crawled about in the most piteous condition on Easter Sunday."[17]

By the Tuesday Newman was ready to give up, despite having noticed a cheering motto in a window of Oriel Hall, *Pie repone te* – "relax". (See Fig. 7. It is actually the motto of Robert Pierreponte, who helped pay for rebuilding the college in the seventeenth century.[18]) Fortunately his old tutor, Thomas Short, having been tipped off by the examiners,

Fig. 7 *The arms of Robert Pierreponte, with the motto which Newman noticed during his examination in Oriel Hall.*

invited him in and encouraged him to continue – this was the occasion of the dinner of lamb cutlets with parsley. There followed three days of oral *viva voce* examinations in the "round room" above the gatehouse. Eventually, on Friday 12th April, "The Provost's Butler, to whom it fell by usage to take the news to the fortunate candidates, made his way to Mr Newman's lodgings in Broad Street, and found him playing the violin. This in itself disconcerted the messenger, who did not associate such an accomplishment with a candidateship for the Oriel Common Room; but his perplexity was increased, when on his delivering what may be supposed to have been his usual form of speech on such occasions, that "he had, he feared, disagreeeable news to announce, viz. that Mr Newman was elected Fellow of Oriel, and that his immediate presence was required there," the person addressed, thinking that such language savoured of impertinent familiarity, merely answered "very well" and went on fiddling. This led the man to ask whether perhaps he had mistaken the rooms and gone to the wrong person, to which Mr Newman replied that it was all right. But, as may be imagined, no sooner had the man left, than he flung down his instrument, and dashed down stairs with all speed to Oriel College. And he recollected after fifty years the eloquent faces and eager bows of the tradesmen and others whom he met on his way, who had heard the news, and well understood why he was crossing from St Mary's to the lane opposite at so extraordinary a pace.[19] Presumably, starting from Seale's, he went along Catte Street past the Bodleian, crossed the High Street by St Mary's and dashed down Oriel Street to the gate of the college – he told his mother that the "Bells were set ringing from three different towers (I had to pay for it)".[20]

Oriel College

And so he came to Oriel (**3** on plan). Oriel was an older college than Trinity, founded in 1324-6 by Adam de Brome and King Edward II, to the memory of which unfortunate monarch Newman was ever loyal. The buildings were completely rebuilt between 1620 and 1642, and are undistinguished, similar to a number of other colleges rebuilt at that time (Fig. 8). Newman was first received in the common room where he was greeted by the intellectual giants of the age, Copleston and Hawkins,

Fig. 8 *The buildings of Oriel College, engraving for John Skelton, 1818.*

Whately and Keble, whose portraits are found with Pusey's and Newman's own on the walls of the room. Common room occupies the ground floor of the elegant Palladian library block, added in 1788 by James Wyatt (Fig. 9). It was the centre of collegiate life, "its members remarkable for the complexion of their theology and their union among themselves in it, as for their literary eminence."[21] Dean Burgon paints a livelier picture, and incidentally reminds us that colourful Regency clothing still kept sober Victorian black at bay: "An aged member of Christ Church . . . declared to the present writer that the only thing he could recall of the Oriel Common-room of that period was a frolicsome tournament on the hearth-rug between two mounted combatants . . . armed with the handscreens which for many a long year used to adorn the mantle-piece." Hawkins reported, "the first time I saw Whately, he wore a pea-green coat, white waistcoat, stone-coloured shorts, flesh-coloured silk stockings. His hair was powdered," while Heber "was dressed in a parsley-and butter coat," and Arnold in "a light blue coat with metal buttons, and a buff waistcoat."[22] Certainly Newman and his young associates spent much time in music-making, and were decidedly light-hearted in their correspondence and vacation amusements, as the *Letters and Diaries* amply testify. Rather surprisingly, ladies were sometimes allowed to dine in Common-room, as his sister Harriett tells us: "We have been dining in O.C. common room . . . Those common rooms are certainly delightful places; I should soon catch cold elsewhere, if used to them."[23]

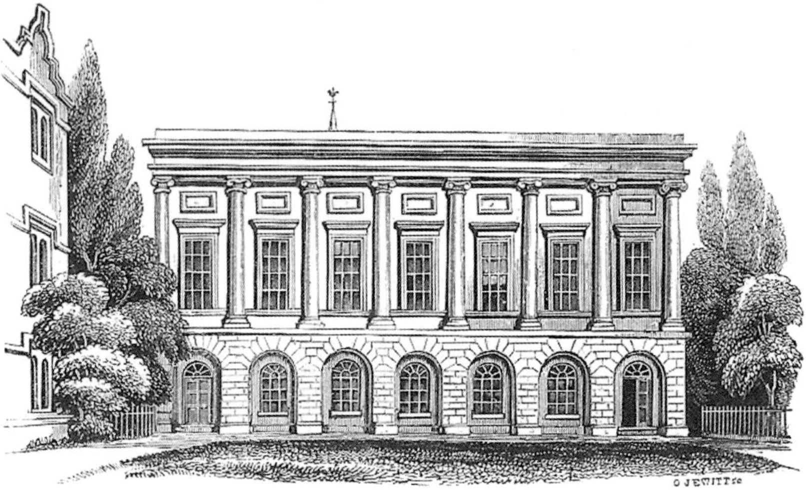

Fig. 9 *The Library and Common-Room at Oriel, woodcut by Jewitt, for Ingram's Memorials.*

From Common-room, Newman was escorted to the **Chapel**, where he was literally installed by being placed in a Fellow's stall for evening prayers. The chapel is one of the less distinguished of Oxford college chapels, retaining its severe mid-seventeenth-century woodwork, without the Baroque exuberance of the later Trinity carvings (Fig. 10). Newman is not particularly associated with this chapel, although he was obliged by the terms of his fellowship to attend service here frequently, and he afterwards served as one of the chaplains for two periods, 1826-31 and 1833-35. He did occasionally spark off "some little controversy" over a sermon.[24] For most of his time as a fellow his clerical duties kept him elsewhere. The chapel service in his time was noted, for "the decorum, the full attendance, the uniformity of response, all delightful",[25] and Newman himself was to

Fig. 10 *Interior of the chapel, Oriel College, in late 19th century. Photograph, National Monuments Record. RCHME © Crown Copyright.*

be emphatic on the value of chapel attendance for the young men.[26]

From chapel they naturally proceeded to the **Hall** for dinner, the scene of Newman's recent written examinations. This could be quite an ordeal in itself – one of Newman's young contemporaries was publicly rebuked by Provost Copleston, "Mr Jelf, we do not carve sweetbread with a spoon.

Manciple, bring a blunt knife."[27] Outside the hall is an extraordinary porch with statues of the Virgin and Child – most daring for the seventeenth century – and two kings presumed to be Edward II and James I. The original inscription, now restored, *Regnante Carolo* – "[built] when Charles was King" – had fallen into decay and throughout Newman's lifetime was replaced by a simple parapet (Fig. 11). Inside, the hall has a fine hammer-beam roof, and portraits of many of the luminaries of Oriel's past – among them we can see Whately, Keble and Newman himself. The panelling is later than Newman's time – Fig. 6 shows it with the earlier woodwork and gas fittings which Newman would have known. In the armorial stained glass in the middle window of the west side is to be found the arms and motto of the Pierreponte family which Newman found so encouraging while he sat for the fellowship exam.

To begin with Newman did not insist on his rights as a fellow, but continued to live in lodgings, waiting until suitable rooms should be available, except in vacation time, when he occupied empty rooms.[28] Despite his earlier misunderstanding with the Provost's Butler, Palmer, he and Frank moved in with him in a house opposite Merton **(2c),** probably on the corner of Magpie Lane. Frank is mistaken in claiming that Blanco White lived with them and played duets with Newman, for Blanco did not appear on the scene until four years later, but his memory is correct that the Dean of Oriel offered to supply Frank's meals until he moved out on winning a place at Worcester College.[29] Newman changed lodgings frequently, spending the autumn of 1823 at "Messenger's lodgings in High Street, a large house," either No. 104 or No. 102 at the corner of Oriel Street **(2d)**. Thence he had to "paddle to dinner in thin shoes and silk stockings" during a wet autumn,[30] so not surprisingly he moved closer to college in the spring, to "Varney's, I think in St Mary Hall Lane, til . . . I removed to Combe's also in St Mary Hall Lane" in the following autumn. The lane is now named Oriel Street **(2e** and **f)** – the only house that can be positively identified is Varney's, now no. 6, part of "Carter House". In January 1825 he moved again to "Hunt's a large house on the same side of the High Street, but further than Messenger's", on the site of the present No. 108 at the corner of King Edward Street **(2g)**. A final move came in the summer of 1825 when he moved to "King's, the Cook's lodgings in the angle of Merton Lane, beyond Merton Garden" **(2h).**

At last, in the spring of 1826, rooms came vacant in college. His colleague R.W. Jelf (the one humiliated over the sweetbreads) left to become tutor to the future King of Hanover, and Newman secured his rooms, "those which of all others I have always wished to have".[31] The rooms are in the main quadrangle, on the south side, the first floor, adjacent to the chapel. The windows face south only, but on the floor above Hurrell Froude was to live in the only rooms with a window facing east, visible at the end of the chapel as it is seen from Merton Street (Fig. 12).

Fig. 11 *Porch of Oriel College Hall as it was in Newman's time, anonymous engraving, mid 19th century.*

Newman's room opened into a curious triangular space tucked behind the chapel organ, and filling the great oriel window overlooking the quad: it actually serves to conceal the change in alignment between the chapel and quad. In the early nineteenth century it was "a nondescript appendage to the set of rooms of which we are speaking; available as a larder, an oratory, or a lumber-closet." Whately, the future Archbishop of Dublin, had lived in these rooms before Jelf and used to keep a string of herrings hanging up in front of the window, from which he "would pull a herring daily . . . and frizzle it for breakfast on the coals of his fire." Charles Marriott told Dean Burgon that when Newman moved in he "found the last of Whately's herrings still hanging on the string before the chapel window." Newman, rather surprisingly, converted it into a shower, which he used every morning (we must remember that without electric light, the interior would have been quite invisible to anyone in the quad at four in the morning).[32] It has now, with more decorum, been converted into a little chapel, recently embellished with painted glass illustrating the life and work of Newman (Fig. 13).

Years later, his young servant or 'scout', John Haycroft, recalled that although "Dr Newman often rose as early as 4 a.m., hot water was not required before 7 a.m. At 8 a.m. he went to St Mary's, then breakfast, followed by a visit to the common room, then work again until luncheon, which his servant often prepared early and placed in the window sill, ready for use when required, Dr Newman then helping himself. The afternoon was generally devoted to walking, and at one period Dr Newman went daily to Rose Hill, to visit his mother and sister. Tea was often made by Dr Newman himself in his room, about 5 p.m. Dinner and common-room would occupy the early hours of the evening, after which there would be more writing. If papers and proofs were ready by 11 p.m. Haycroft would see to their despatch, but if it was much later before they were finished, Dr Newman would go out again himself."[33] Dean Burgon tells

Fig. 12. *Oriel chapel from Merton Street, with Froude's window above Newman's rooms visible beyond the last bay of the chapel. Woodcut by Jewitt for Ingram's Memorials.*

Fig. 13 *The space behind the chapel organ, before the installation of the new painted glass. Photograph by Stephen Humphreys.*

us that the rooms were "ill-carpeted and indifferently furnished, as well as encumbered with book-shelves in every part."[34] Actually Newman had paid £103 for the furniture he found in the rooms, so it cannot have been that indifferent.[35] In these rooms Newman was to remain until his final departure from college.

Dean advancing asked *'Quis adest?'* 'Please sir.' (replied a tremulous voice), 'it's me, the college washerwoman.' The gate was opened, and between the Fellows, drawn up in two ranks, passed a venerable matron laden with baskets of clean linen."[36] The college gate opens onto Oriel Square, from which may be seen the great tower and spire of St Mary's, the parish which Edward Hawkins had to relinquish on becoming Provost, and which he was to hand on to Newman (Fig. 14).

St Clement's Church

A fellow of an Oxford college before the mid-nineteenth-century upheavals was not necessarily expected to teach or lecture and was free to pursue any compatible vocation, in particular that of pastoral care. Newman decided in May 1824 to accept a curacy. "St Clement's Church is to be rebuilt – but, before beginning the subscriptions, it is proposed, Gutch the Rector being incapacitated through age, to provide a Curate, who shall be a kind of guarantee to the subscribers that every exertion will be made, when the Church is built, to recover the parish from meeting houses, and on the other

Fig. 15 *St Clement's old church, shortly before its demolition in 1826, woodcut by Thomas Fisher for Ingram's Memorials.*

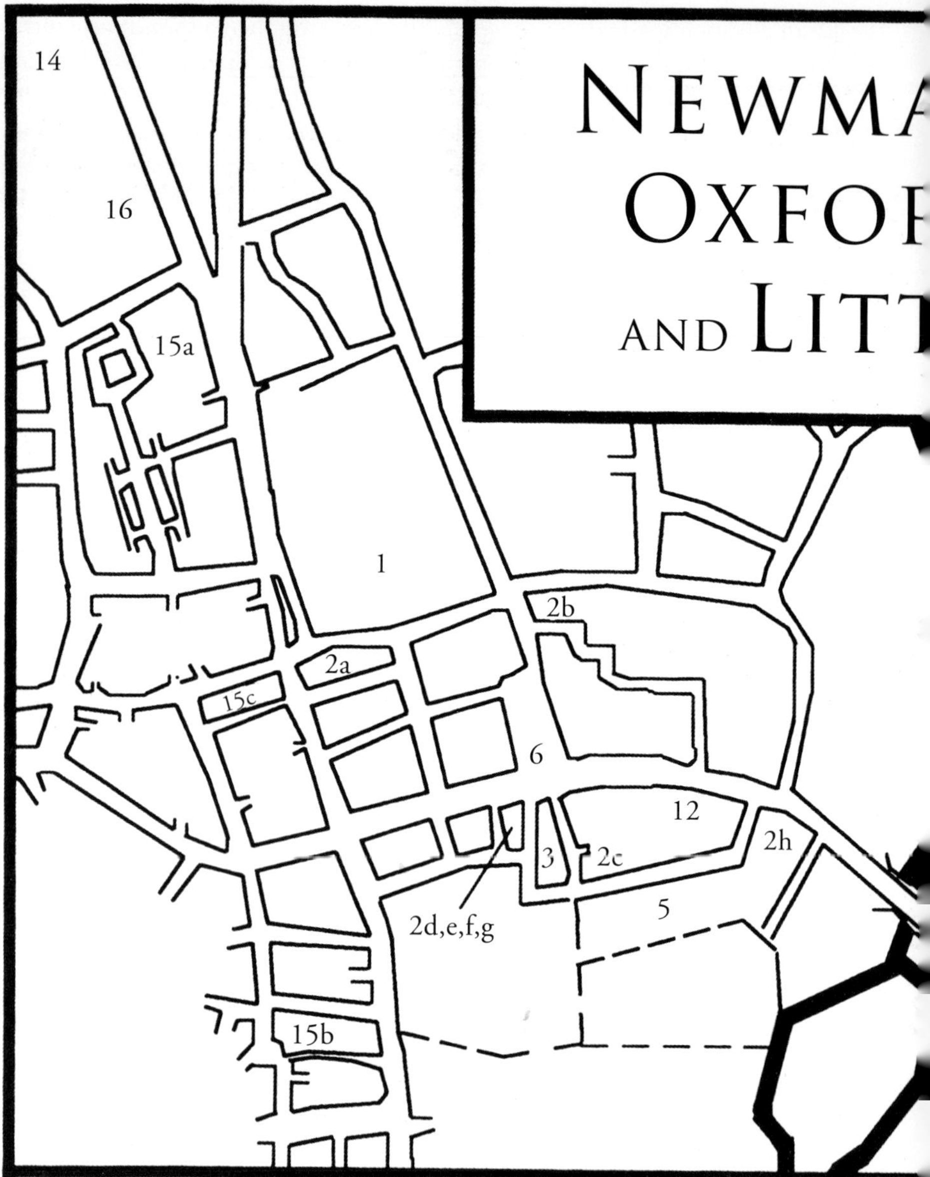

1. Trinity College
5. St Alban Hall
14. The Observatory
2. Newman's Lodgings
6. St Mary the Virgin
15. Proposed Sites for the Oratory

N’S
D
EMORE

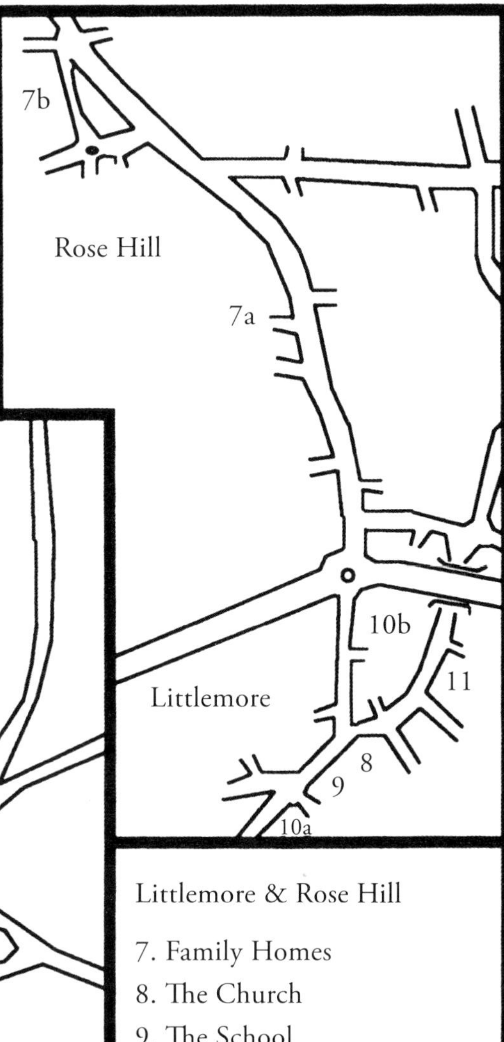

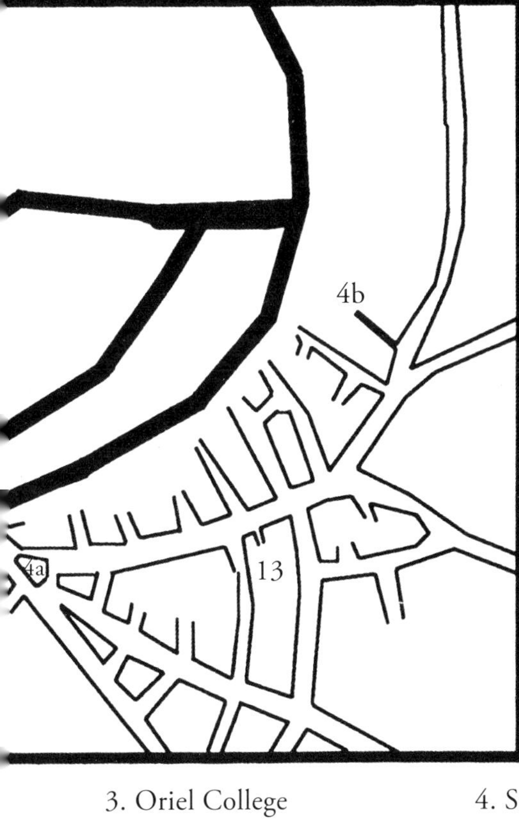

Littlemore & Rose Hill

7. Family Homes
8. The Church
9. The School
10. Newman’s Lodgings
11. The College

3. Oriel College
4. St Clement’s Church
12. The Angel
13. St Ignatius
16. The Oratory

Fig. 16 *St Clement's new church from Magdalen water walks, engraving by Mackenzie, for Ingram's Memorials.*

hand alehouses, into which they had been driven by the want of convenient Sunday worship."[37] To this end he was ordained deacon in Christ Church on 13 June 1824. St Clement's (**4** on plan, Fig. 15) was a ramshackle mediæval building standing immediately across Magdalen Bridge and serving a poor area of mean streets huddled under the slopes of Headington Hill. The Rector, John Gutch, was an elderly antiquary, who was glad to leave the care of the people to his energetic curate. Newman rapidly visited every home in the parish, including that of the Catholic priest, Robert Newsham, who tended an impoverished flock from a tiny hidden chapel (doubtless classed by Newman at that time as one of the "meeting houses").

Newman's energy showed itself in campaigning against Sunday shopping, and in reorganising the church music, provoking a mass walk-out by the choir, who protested they "would rather stay away from Church altogether . . . the Singers, they are all respectable householders of this Parish and have sung ever since they have been able to sing, and they hearing you say that you intended to turn the singers off altogether . . . very strange that a YOUNG CURATE should so show his authority over *an old Rector*."[38] Despite the plans to demolish the church completely, Newman also installed a stove (presented to him by Pusey) as the first heating in the church, and he erected a gallery for Sunday school.

It fell to Newman also to raise the funds for the new church which was eventually built in 1828 in a secluded site off the Marston Road **(4b)**. "He held it [the curacy] long enough to succeed in collecting the £5000 or £6000 which were necessary for the new Church. It was consecrated after he had relinquished his curacy, probably in the Long Vacation, when he was away from Oxford; but so it happened by a singular accident that, neither while it was building, nor after it was built, was he ever inside it. He had no part in determining its architectural character, which was in the hands of a committee."[39] This last exonerates Newman from any responsibility for the stark structure, described by one contemporary as looking like "a boiled rabbit" (Fig. 16). The foundation stone was laid on 11 July 1825, on a Monday – "on Tuesday the work stopped, owing to a fresh rumpus – and the workmen were all sent away. I convened a Committee Wednesday Morning at the wish of the Churchwardens, and the work recommenced on Thursday."[40] The site of the old church **(4a)** is marked only by a patch of grass in the roundabout called "The Plain" and an enigmatic stone which tells us that Peace was declared in Oxford on 27 June 1814.

St Alban Hall

In March 1825 Richard Whately, a former fellow of Oriel, was appointed Principal of St Alban Hall (number **5** on plan) and asked Newman to assist him as Vice-Principal. Newman accepted on the grounds that he ought to be doing something academic as well as parochial. St Alban's was one of the few surviving mediæval Halls, a tiny society of only some dozen undergraduates, always closely associated with the adjacent Merton College, which was to absorb it completely in 1881. All that survives of the building known to Newman is the façade, built in 1599 (Fig. 17). The work involved being "factotum, as Tutor, Chaplain, Bursar, and Dean". "The same room was chapel, hall and lecture room. Whately arranged that I should dine with the men three times a week. I had lectures for the men every day, being the only Tutor and Dean. I read the Prayers on Sunday tho' I had St Clement's duty."[41] During the summer of 1825 Whately allowed Newman's recently widowed mother, and his three sisters, to lodge in the Principal's home, for during this period Whately and Newman were firm friends and

Fig. 17 *St Alban Hall, from Merton Street, engraving by N. Whittock, 1828.*

thought alike – "I think him an excellent man".[42] They were to drift further and further apart until twenty five years later Whately, now Archbishop, refused to meet Newman in Dublin.

For about a year Newman overworked himself with St Clement's and St Alban Hall, choosing the "King's lodging" **(2h)** because it lay between them, but suffering from "a continual wear on my mind, forgetting, mislaying memoranda, names etc."[43] At Easter 1826 he made a complete break, resigned both offices, and accepted the post of Tutor at Oriel, for which he was able to move at last into college.

St Mary's

On 12 March 1828 Edward Hawkins became Provost of Oriel and thus had to vacate the post of Vicar of St Mary's, the University Church (**6** on plan). Newman succeeded him two days later. Hawkins' last act as Vicar had been the triumphant re-opening of the church after a major refitting on 2 March: the new work was serenaded with Attwood's "I was glad", a sermon, Handel's "Lift up your Hearts", a Benedictus by Mozart, and Handel's "Hallelujah Chorus". Newman thus found a church in excellent condition, and a living choral tradition. His own first contribution in 1829 was to instal gas lighting

Fig. 18 *St Mary the Virgin seen from the High Street, engraving by Mackenzie for Ingram's Memorials.*

– some of the fittings can still be seen in the choir, converted for electricity.[44] The building (Fig. 18) is substantially of the fifteenth century, high, light and spacious. Hawkins installed new pews and galleries to accommodate a large congregation in the nave and aisles. All the benches were turned to face the

Fig. 19 *Interior of St Mary the Virgin, June 1833, engraving by Mackenzie for Ingram's Memorials.*

pulpit, and a gallery along the north side was designed for undergraduates, so that they would be on eye-level with the preacher. The new pulpit was to be the stage for Newman's glory, on the hundreds of occasions when he preached for his parishioners, as well as a rather more limited number of occasions when he was chosen to be the University preacher (Fig. 19). There were hardly any parishioners, of course, for the tiny city-centre parish was almost entirely built over by colleges, but the church was packed with people from all over Oxford, and both undergraduates and fellows of the colleges. The engraving on the front cover shows the dignitaries gathering for a University Sermon some time in the 1830s.

Newman's preaching became one of the great attractions of Oxford, and his inimitable style was clearly remembered and recorded forty years later: "To those who are justly penetrated with the force and beauty of these printed sermons, we can only say with Æschines, 'What if you had heard himself pronounce it?' And yet nothing could at first sight be more opposite to the manner of the great Athenian orator. Action in the common sense of the word there was none. Through many of them the preacher never moved anything but his head. His hands were literally not seen from the beginning to the end. The sermon began in a calm musical voice, the key slightly rising as it went on; by-and-by the preacher warmed with his subject, it seemed as if his very soul and body glowed with suppressed emotion. There were times when, in the midst of the most thrilling passages, he would pause, without dropping his voice, for a moment which seemed long, before he uttered with gathered force and solemnity a few weighty words. The very tones of his voice seemed as if they were something more than his own. There are those who to this day in reading many of his sermons have the whole scene brought back before them. The great church, the congregation all breathless with expectant attention. The gaslight just at the left hand of the pulpit, lowered that the preacher might not be dazzled; themselves, perhaps, standing in the half darkness under the gallery, and then the pause before those words in the 'Ventures of Faith' (vol. iv) thrilled through them – 'They say unto him, We are able' . . .

"Nor should the manner of reading the Psalms and the Scripture lessons in the service which preceded the sermon be passed over. Its chief characteristics were the same. Why is it that, while many things at the time even more impressive have faded from the memory, one scene, or perhaps one cadence, remains fixed in it for life? Thus it is that one who more than forty years ago stood just before him almost a boy in the college chapel, has at this moment in his ears the sound of the words, 'Oh, magnify the Lord our God and worship Him upon His holy hill – *for the Lord our God, is Holy.*'"[45] In contrast, the

Rev. J. Clark of Philadelphia stated : "He is a thin sallow-looking man and appears as cold in the pulpit as an icicle. . . . Mr Newman did not in his sermon exhibit any of his particular views. The discourse upon the whole was exceedingly dull and uninteresting." Newman commented on this "the impression produced on an intelligent foreigner, perfectly impartial".[46]

Fig. 20 *Newman in the pulpit of St Mary's, anonymous etching, c. 1835.*

His popularity was such that many little amateur sketches of him were etched and hawked about the streets with titles like "a sketch from memory" or "a sketch from St Mary's". Most show him in his surplice and hood, which he wore to conduct the communion service; in the pulpit he wore only his black University gown (Fig. 20), for "the pulpit of St Mary's was never invaded by the surplice," as Henry Wilberforce remembered. He went on, "It would be a mistake to imagine that during the earlier years there was the least jealousy on the part of the authorities . . . Nay, there were colleges which gave the strongest possible proof of their wish that their members should attend Mr Newman's preaching. The afternoon services began at 4 pm. And the colleges dined at five . . . we have heard that there were colleges which at this time changed their hour on purpose to allow their men to attend St Mary's without deserting the [dining] hall."[47]

Gradually, as Newman's doctrine developed, he introduced or revived services unfamiliar to early-nineteenth-century Anglicans. He began the daily service of Matins and Evensong in 1834, and on Easter Day 1837 started the unprecedented custom of celebrating communion every Sunday. "I found the Church very well attended. I have it at seven in the morning. Last Sunday I had thirty-six communicants."[48] This communion service was held in the chancel, where the original fifteenth-century choir stalls survive around the walls. The worshippers remained in the stalls, and the bread and wine were brought round to them, indicating that the numbers attending can never have rivalled the crowds who came to the preaching services in the nave. Here too, under the sanctuary, Newman was to bury his mother.

As well as the Sunday sermons, a usual part of parish life at the time was "lectures" on weekdays. Newman began giving these in the chancel, until in 1834 he cleaned out the fourteenth-century chapel of Adam de Brome, one of the founders of Oriel, and equipped it as a lecture room. At that time it was completely walled off from the church, approached by a door under the tower (now blocked by an altar), and had been neglected and disused for years. Here he gave Wednesday night talks, which were attended mostly by members of the University, and at which he developed the theology of the apostolical movement. The first lecture was attended by a hundred men, among them W.G. Ward, "a fat but very clever young man from Balliol, whose fixed stare so put Newman off that he had the benches arranged a different way."[49] In 1932 the chapel was opened into the main church, so that it now appears to be an outer north aisle, but Newman's desk and the benches survive on three sides. It was in 1932 also that the undergraduates' gallery over the north aisle was demolished. At the same time some of the benches in the nave, which originally faced the pulpit, were turned to face east. More recently a space was cleared at the east end of the nave for a moveable altar platform.

Newman's influence and fame were at their peak during the fifteen years he served St Mary's, the years of the Tracts, of the translations of the Fathers, of the sermons, Parochial and Plain, in short of the 'Oxford Movement' which was to transform the ecclesiastical world. Following a disagreement with Provost Hawkins, he resigned his post as Tutor at Oriel in 1830, and had few further duties there. The work at St Mary's expanded rapidly, and in 1829 he had to appoint a curate, Isaac Williams, whose portrait we have seen in Trinity. Despite himself, the University crowded in on his pastoral work: "I think I may say truly that I have begun scarcely any plan but for the sake of my parish, but every one has turned, independently of me, into the direction of the University. I began Saints'-days Services, daily Services, and Lectures in Adam de Brome's chapel, for my parishioners, but they have not come to them. . . . The Weekly Communion, I believe, I did begin for the sake of the University."[50] A growing feature of Newman's spirituality was his appreciation of the role of the Blessed Virgin Mary in the Church, which was certainly furthered by the dedication to her of both his college and his parish, and the statues of her on both buildings. That over the porch of St Mary's was a cause of conflict in the Civil War, but is still there, probably the only post-Reformation statue of Our Lady to have survived in a prominent position in a public street in England (Fig. 21).

Fig. 21 *The Porch of St Mary the Virgin, with statue of the Blessed Virgin, lithograph by A. Pugin for Ackermann, 1818.*

LITTLEMORE

Newman was still eager for pastoral work among the poor, and devoted much time to the obscure hamlet of Littlemore, three miles from Oxford, which by some quirk of parochial history came under the care of St Mary's. From his first appointment to St Mary's, he visited the people assiduously, catechised the children, and began to think of building a school and chapel for them. In his pastoral work he was aided by his mother and surviving sisters. They had come in 1828 to stay near Oxford at Nuneham Courtenay, and from the summer of 1829 decided to live near Oxford, first at Horspath and then back at Nuneham, before settling in autumn 1830 at Rose Hill, on the way from Oxford to Littlemore. They rented two cottages on the crest of the hill (number **7a** on plan). This had the effect of providing a holiday home for Newman, "John has taken possession of his new apartments – consisting of a hall, staircase, study and bedroom – quite grand is he not? His study is very pretty and comfortable for summer. We have made a new large window in it, allowing him a view of our garden, and a very pleasant look out towards Oxford. . . . He has just begun his hard reading for a book he has undertaken to write."[51] They stayed here nearly three years before buying the larger house now called **Grove House** (number **7b** on plan, Fig. 22) in the spring of 1833, where they were to live until Mrs Newman's death. (Confusingly, Newman continued

Fig. 22 *Grove House, Iffley, c. 1895. Photograph by Henry Taunt.*
© Images & Voices, Oxfordshire County Council.

to refer to the new house as "Rose Hill" although the ladies called it "Rose Bank". More recently the house was owned and cherished by Mrs Graham Greene.)

Mrs Newman and the girls "attended to the schools, the charities, and the sick people of Littlemore, which though without a church, and at that time with scarcely a genteel residence, had more care bestowed on it than many a village furnished with all the outward symbols of parochial completeness."[52]

When the cholera arrived in 1831 the Newmans set up Rose Hill as a Head-Quarters for nurses and Depot of Medicines. Newman wrote to his brother Frank, "How can I manage a parish without women?" and forty years later the family were remembered as "ideals of goodness and taste . . . she was of your mother's class, has most devoted recollections of her kindness to people, knows still her taste in needlework, and how particular she was."[53]

The longed-for **Church at Littlemore** (number **8** on plan, Fig. 23) was begun in 1835, and Newman's mother laid the first stone during general festivities. Yet before it was completed she herself was laid to rest in the vault

Fig. 23 *The church at Littlemore, from Ingram's Memorials.*

of St Mary's church. She is commemorated by a tablet at Littlemore, showing the incomplete chapel behind her. It was carved by Newman's school friend Richard Westmacott the Younger, who also produced a fine bust of Newman himself. The church was consecrated on 22 September 1836, a day Newman kept as a significant anniversary for years. It was severely plain but beautifully proportioned, and the plans were published by the Architectural Society as a model for small village churches. The flowers, cloths and other ornaments were the object of much devotion, and although unobjectionable by modern standards, were considered dangerously ritualistic at the time. "We have got some roses, wall-flowers and sweet-briar, and the chapel smells as if to remind one of the Holy Sepulchre."[54] On the anniversary in September 1842 the procession attracted protest, "there was a vulgar stranger there, making a noise, crying Popish, etc . . . the little man must have calmed down, for the sermon was preached without disturbance."[55]

The following year the anniversary was to be the occasion for Newman's last Anglican sermon, the "Parting of Friends". Pusey wrote of it: "The sermon was like one of Newman's in which self was altogether repressed, yet it showed the more how deeply he felt the misconception of himself. It implied rather than said farewell. People sobbed audibly, and I, who officiated at the altar, could hardly help mingling sorrow with even that Feast. However 'the peace of God which surpasseth all understanding' closed all."[56] Two weeks later Newman celebrated the holy communion for the last time. "Some who were present in the gloom of that early October morning felt that they were assisting at the funeral of a religious effort that had failed."[57]

The next of Newman's building projects was the **village school** (number **9** on plan, seen clearly in the foreground of Fig. 24), the scene of much of Newman's work. It was actually built under the direction of his eager curate, J.R. Bloxam, who came to live in Littlemore in 1837 and built the school a year later.[58] It remained in use as the village school until the 1990s. We must not think of Newman as a remote academic, for he was fully involved in the life of the semi-civilised children of "this wild neighbourhood".[59] Yet even here his university followers found him out: "Newman's catechizing being a great attraction this Lent. Men have gone out of Oxford every Sunday to hear it . . . very striking, done with much spirit, and the children so up to it, answering with much alacrity." "I have been reforming, or at least lecturing against uncombed hair, and dirty faces and hands; but I find I am not deep in the philosophy of school-girl tidiness". "I despair almost. The top girls hardly know Adam from Noah". "Can you suggest any method of bringing children punctual . . . The children are improving in their singing. I have had the audacity to lead them and teach them some new tunes. Also I have rummaged out a violin and strung it . . . I have just begun chanting, Gregorian chant which the children seem to take to . . . I have effected a great reform (for the time) in the girls' hands and faces – lectured with unblushing effrontery on the necessity of their keeping *their work clean* and set them to knit stockings with all their might. Also I am going to give them some clean white pinafores."[60]

Newman had already begun to prefer staying in Littlemore to his rooms in Oriel: in Lent 1840 he lodged with Bloxam, at the 'George' inn (**10a**), and in early 1841 he stayed at a house called 'St George's' (**10b**) which had once been used by recusant Catholics. He bought land for a possible residence and planted it with trees, but eventually settled for an old granary turned into cottages (number **11** on plan) which he was able to lease on 29 September 1841 at first as an occasional retreat, but after February 1842 as his home, and a home for those who would share it with him. It became the object of much speculation, the butt of much satire, being compared with the newly established Irish seminary of Maynooth, and considered, as in fact it was, but a stage on the path to Oscott, Bishop Wiseman's flourishing new seminary near Birmingham (Fig. 24). Jestingly Newman called it a μονή, which had hidden meanings. In Classical Greek it means simply a 'dwelling', and he was able to tell the bishop it was just "a parsonage house for Littlemore".[61] In Church Greek it means a 'monastery', and he told his close friend Maria Giberne it was "a half college half monastery".[62] Indeed the silent scholarly way of life of his associates was stricter than many monasteries, as Blessed Dominic Barberi tells us: "To pass from one cell to another you must go through a little outside corridor, covered indeed with tiles, but open to all inclemencies of the weather . . . In the cells, nothing is to be seen but poverty and

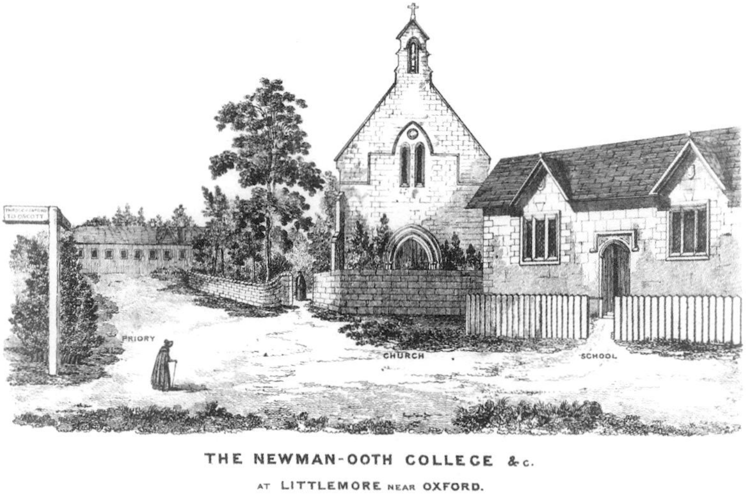

Fig. 24 *Satirical drawing of Newman's school, church and college at Littlemore compared to Maynooth College, and with the road to Oscott indicated, c. 1844. Bodleian Library, MS G.A. Oxon, a.77, fo. 60v, lower.*

simplicity . . . no delicacies, no wine, no liquors, and seldom meat . . . A Capuchin monastery would appear a great palace when compared with Littlemore."[63] But in Patristic Greek, it had a special meaning of a 'place of transit', a staging post, as indeed it was to be Newman's place of transit from Oxford to Birmingham. It was while living in Littlemore that Newman edited some of the works of his favourite saint Athanasius, and made a footnote to that effect.[64]

At one end was the library, housing his incomparable collection of the writings of the Fathers. At the other was his own room, which has been furnished to match as closely as possible the style and austerity of his time, by Fr Humphrey Carpenter of the Birmingham Oratory, with assistance from Mrs Graham Greene. Beyond that is the little chapel, also now restored and once again hung with red. The place was perhaps not quite as austere as Blessed Dominic implies, for one of the young men, John Dalgairns, said: "Newman declares his object is not to teach people austerities, but only living in a plain, frugal way, so as to get out of the gentleman-parson line. . . . Each set of rooms was originally intended for a cottage for poor people to live in; but now what with bookcases, sundry (Roman) prints and so on, have really an air of – what shall I call it, poor-gentleman-likeness about them, quite romantic."[65]

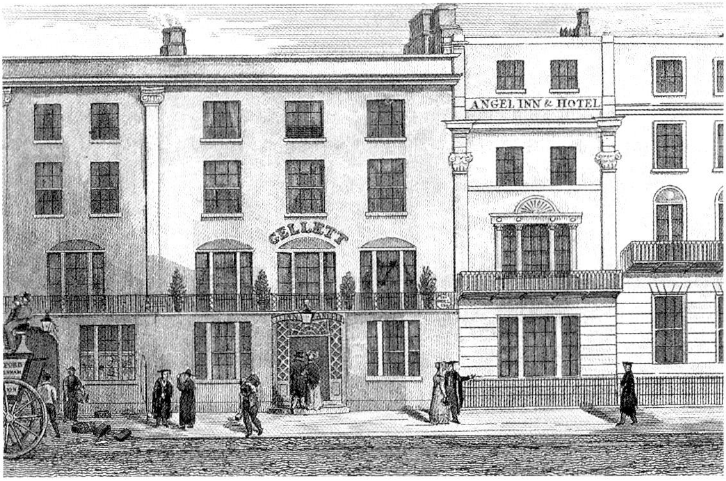

Fig. 25 *The Angel Hotel in Oxford High Street, with passengers just arrived off a coach. Engraving by J. Bridges, c. 1845.*

Here the last scenes of Newman's Oxford life were to be played out. Here visitors came and went, here he studied and wrote. One by one his followers slipped away, either to be received quietly into the Catholic Church, like John Dalgairns, or to return to Oxford, respectability and career, like Mark Pattison. Eventually, on 8th October 1845, word came that the extraordinary Passionist missionary Blessed Dominic Barberi was coming to visit Littlemore at the invitation of Dalgairns. He arrived from Staffordshire on the top of the coach, in pouring rain, and alighted at the Angel Hotel in the High Street (number **12** on the plan), where Dalgairns was waiting for him. (Most of the Angel is still standing, next to the Examination Schools, Fig. 25.) After a brief stop at the hotel, they took a cab to Littlemore, where Newman fell on his knees before the missionary, begging to be received into the one fold of the Redeemer. On the morning of the 9th October, now his feast-day, Newman made his first Catholic Communion at a Mass celebrated in the little chapel, on the writing desk which is now in the library. "O Englishmen, hear the voice of Littlemore! Those walls bear testimony that the Catholic is a little more than the Protestant Church, the soul a little more than the body, eternity a little more than time."[66]

The following Sunday Newman and a little group of his associates walked down the hill to the obscure **Chapel of St Ignatius** in the suburb

Fig. 26 *The Catholic chapel and priest's house in St Clement's High Street, c. 1840. Bodleian Library, MS G.A. Oxon, a.69, fo. 116.*

of St Clement's (number **13** on plan, Fig. 26) where Robert Newsham still ministered as Catholic priest. For a few months Newman continued to be based at Littlemore, and attended Mass in this chapel twice a week, while the preparations were made for him to pursue his vocation in the Catholic Church. It was an uneasy time: "It is a great trial to remain where there are no outward tokens or means of Catholic communion. It is said that the one support to persons in my case has been the daily Mass – now Mass is only twice a week at St Clement's, and at a distance of 2 or 3 miles. Nor is it a slight trial, as you may suppose, except as faith overcomes it, to go to what to outward appearance is a meeting house."[67]

At last, in February 1846, everything was packed up, and Newman was left alone in the empty buildings at Littlemore. For his last night he accepted an invitation from an old friend, the astronomer Johnson. So it came about that it was the Observatory (**14**, Fig. 27) that he was to leave on the morning of the 23rd, not to see Oxford again for many years, save only its spires as they are seen from the railway.

Fig. 27 *The Radcliffe Observatory, engraving by Mackenzie for Ingram's Memorials.*

A Return

But there is a postscript to the story of Newman's association with his beloved Oxford. Between 1864 and 1867 three attempts were made by William Bernard Ullathorne, the Bishop of Birmingham and responsible for Oxford, to bring Newman's Oratorians to Oxford, for the pastoral care of the people, if not yet of the University. Newman by now was well established as the Father of the Birmingham Oratory, shown in a portrait of this period as still alert and pensive, though his hair was grey (back cover). Powerful interests in Westminster and Rome were to quash the Oxford scheme, but not before Newman had three times acquired land for the project. The first site was the old city Workhouse **(15a)**, an impressive eighteenth-century building, standing in large grounds with its own cemetery (Fig. 28); Wellington Square was later built on the site. The second site, for which plans were at one stage well advanced, was in St Aldate's Street near the present University Catholic Chaplaincy **(15b)**. The third site, which Newman felt was the best located, was in St Michael's Street, now the Northgate Hall **(15c)**.

It was not until 1878, after the Oratory scheme had been laid to rest,

Fig. 28 *The Workhouse off Walton Street, drawing by J. Buckley, 1827. Bodleian Library, MS Don. a.3, fo. 119.*

that Newman at last came back to Oxford, for that reception as Honorary Fellow of Trinity already described. On that occasion he called on Pusey, whom he found "much older" and saw the "magnificent buildings which they have erected" as Keble College.[68] Two years later he returned as a Cardinal, once again to dine in Trinity on the occasion of their gaudy, Trinity Sunday 1880. This time he preached both morning and evening at the newly built Jesuit church "with something of his wonted fire and sweetness in the Oxford pulpit."[69] A sketch done at the time shows him in the old wooden pulpit of St Aloysius, and was completed by drawing the young Newman in St Mary's pulpit and surrounding the figures with views of the various buildings of his Oxford career (title page).

Newman, you might think, had been vindicated in his Oxford. Yet when he died in 1890 the proposal to erect a public memorial to him was angrily repudiated by the city and University – a protest meeting was held in the Town Hall, and one of the speakers asked scornfully, "Has Newman done anything to bring honour to Oxford?"[70] Even sixteen years later, when Cecil Rhodes wished to decorate his new building for Oriel with college worthies, the statue of Newman was, as we have seen, hidden on the inside wall.

It was not until Newman had been dead a hundred years that the Oratory finally arrived in Oxford, using the former Jesuit church of St Aloysius **(16)**. Here Newman's Congregation of the Oratory were at last established as pastors and scholars, ministering to the liturgy, the sacrament of penance, the instruction of the many converts who follow Newman's path into the Catholic Church. The church, designed by Joseph Hansom and opened in 1875, has become a centre where people come all day long to pray, and the adjacent house soon showed itself to be too small for the increasing work of the community. Here, then, Oxford's Newman has returned to take his rightful place in Blessed John Henry Newman's Oxford.

Visiting Newman's Oxford

1. Trinity College is usually open to visitors between 2 and 5 of an afternoon, though during the summer months an admission charge is usually made. Visitors may enter the hall and chapel, and pass through the quadrangles and the garden.

2. Of Newman's lodgings, few can be located with certainty – Messenger's (2d) is either 102 or 104, High Street, both now shops. Varney's (2e) is number 6, Oriel street. The first Broad Street lodgings (2a) and Combe's in Oriel Street (2f) could be any of several properties: the outsides of all these are visible from the public street. Seal's (2b), Palmer's (2c), Hunt's (2g), and King's (2h) have been demolished and replaced with later buildings.
3. Oriel College is not normally open to the public, although during University term the quadrangles may sometimes be seen: to visit other parts of the college, application should be made in writing to the Bursar.
4. Of old St Clement's there is nothing to see. The new church lies back from the Marston Road, and is not open except for services.
5. The only part of St Alban Hall remaining from Newman's day is the street front visible only from Merton Street, though Merton College is usually open in the afternoons.
6. The University Church is open every day and may be visited except during services. A view of the city is available from the top of the Tower.
7. Grove House (7b) and the cottages at the top of Rose Hill (7a) are private, but can be glimpsed from the street.
8. Littlemore Church is not usually open except for services, but the key can often be obtained from the college.
9. Littlemore School can be seen from the road. At the time of writing it is still boarded up, and its future is uncertain.
10. The George at Littlemore (10a) is open during licensing hours; St George's House (10b) can be seen from Cowley Road near the College.
11. Newman's retreat, known as the College, Littlemore, is now the International Centre of Newman Friends, run by the sisters of the Spiritual Family 'The Work'. It is open on request daily: Monday to Friday 10:30 to 12 and 2 to 5; Saturday and Sunday (except the last Sunday of the month) 2 to 5. The library, chapel and Newman's room are shown to visitors. (For groups, apply in advance, 01865-779743).
12. The former Angel Hotel is now shops, open to prospective purchasers.
13. St Ignatius' Chapel is now an office: the outside may be seen from the street.
14. The Radcliffe Observatory, a fine but little known building, is now part of Green Templeton College. It will form the central feature of the

new University area being constructed on the site of the former hospital.
15. Of the three sites proposed for the Oxford Oratory only the second (15b) still retains the buildings Newman bought, on the corner of St Aldate's and Brewer Streets. The massive enclosure wall of the Workhouse (15a) can be glimpsed behind some properties in Wellington Square.
16. The existing Oxford Oratory Church is open daily from 7 am to 7 pm (except for an hour or so on Sunday afternoon) and is in constant use for public or private prayer.

There are frequent buses from Oxford city centre to Littlemore: the Minchery Farm bus stops outside the College, but takes a roundabout route to get there; it is usually quicker to get a Rose Hill bus and walk the last few hundred metres.

Times of opening and details of accessibility are of course subject to change.

NOTES

1 *Autobiographical Writings*, 30.
2 *Letters and Diaries*, I, 35, 11 June 1817.
3 *Letters and Diaries*, I, 40, 27 June 1817.
4 Wilfrid Ward, II, 429-30.
5 *Apologia*, 327.
6 *Verses on Various Occasions*, 13-15.
7 *Letters and Diaries*, XXV, 105-7, 22 April 1870. *Trinity College Newsletter*, Winter 2007, 4.
8 *Letters and Diaries*, I, 70, 10 December 1819.
9 *Letters and Diaries*, I, 37, 16 June 1817.
10 *Autobiographical Writings*, 156-7; *Apologia*, 327.
11 *Letters and Diaries*, I, 48, note to 30 November 1817.
12 *Letters and Diaries* XXIV, 77, 22 May 1868.
13 *Letters and Diaries*, I, 135.
14 Howard Colvin, *Unbuilt Oxford* (New Haven and London 1983), 60.
15 *Letters and Diaries*, I, 110, 25 June 1821.
16 *Letters and Diaries*, I, 131, 13 April 1822.
17 *Letters and Diaries*, I, 132, 15 April 1822.
18 Anthony Wood, *The History and Antiquities of the Colleges and Halls in the University of Oxford*, ed. R. Gutch, 1786, 130.
19 *Letters and Diaries*, I, 127, note.
20 *Letters and Diaries*, I, 110, 3 May 1822 (I can find no other evidence for the bell-ringing).
21 *Autobiographical Writings*, 73.
22 Burgon, *Twelve Good Men*, 199-200.
23 *Newman Family Letters*, 91.
24 *Autobiographical Writings*, 211
25 Burgon, *Twelve Good Men*, 212
26 *Letters and Diaries*, I, 152, 22 September 1822.
27 *Letters and Diaries*, II, 181 (the story has been told of Newman himself).
28 These moves are chronicled in *Letters and Diaries*, I, 135-6.
29 *Letters and Diaries*, I, 135, 156; F.W. Newman, *Early Life*, 13-14.
30 *Letters and Diaries*, I, 110, 11 November 1823.
31 *Letters and Diaries*, I, 280, 21 March 1826.
32 Burgon, *Twelve Good Men*, 201; *Letters and Diaries*, II, 260, 29 July 1830.
33 T. Squires, *In West Oxford* (London and Oxford 1928), 125.
34 Burgon, *Twelve Good Men*, 201 – the Dean is mistaken in supposing that

Newman directly succeeded Whately in the rooms.
35 *Letters and Diaries*, I, 110, 1 April 1826.
36 Burgon, *Twelve Good Men*, 209.
37 *Autobiographical Writings*, 198-9.
38 *Letters and Diaries*, I, 233, about 27 May 1825.
39 *Autobiographical Writings*, 72.
40 *Letters and Diaries*, I, 243, 16 July 1825.
41 *Letters and Diaries*, I, 228, 16 April 1825, and 280, 21 March 1826.
42 *Autobiographical Writings*, 209.
43 *Autobiographical Writings*, 208.
44 T.G. Jackson, *The Church of St Mary the Virgin, Oxford* (Oxford, 1897), 143; Oxfordshire Record Office, PAR 209/4/F1/123, accounts for 1829.
45 Anne Mozley, *Letters and Correspondance*, II, 219.
46 Maisie Ward, *Young Mr Newman*, 318.
47 Henry Wilberforce's reminiscences, in *Letters and Diaries* XXXII, 536, 538.
48 *Young Mr Newman*, 314.
49 Meriol Trevor, *Newman's Journey*, 63.
50 *Apologia*, 229.
51 *Newman Family Letters*, 36-7.
52 *Young Mr Newman*, 174.
53 *Young Mr Newman*, 269-70.
54 *Young Mr Newman*, 364.
55 *Young Mr Newman*, 392.
56 *Young Mr Newman*, 400.
57 Geoffrey Faber, *Oxford Apostles*, (London, 1933), 438.
58 Middleton, *Newman and Bloxam*, 38.
59 *Newman Family Letters*, 52.
60 *Young Mr Newman*, 361-2.
61 *Letters and Diaries*, VIII, 506, 14 April 1842.
62 *Letters and Diaries* VIII, 497, 30 March 1842.
63 Young, *Venerable Father Dominic*, 265.
64 JHN (ed.), *Historical Tracts of S. Athanasius*, Library of the Fathers, Oxford, 1843, 50, note h.
65 *Newman and Bloxam*, 88.
66 *Venerable Father Dominic*, 265.
67 *Letters and Diaries*, XI, 16, 14 October 1845.
68 Wilfrid Ward, II, 431.
69 C.C. Martindale, *Catholics in Oxford* (Oxford, 1925), 30.
70 Drawings for the *Illustrated London News*, in possession of the Oxford Oratory.

Sources and Further Reading

John Henry Newman, *Apologia pro Vita Sua*, London, 1864, frequently reprinted.

Autobiographical Writings, ed. Henry Tristram, London & New York, 1956.

Letters and Diaries, 32 volumes, originally edited by Charles Stephen Dessain, London and Oxford, 1978 to 2008.

Verses on Various Occasions, 1868.

John Burgon, *Lives of Twelve Good Men*, London, 1891.

R.D. Middleton, *Newman and Bloxam*, Oxford, 1947.

Anne Mozley, *Letters and Correspondence of John Henry Newman*, 2 Vols, London, 1891.

Dorothea Mozley (ed.), *Newman Family Letters*, London, 1962.

F.W. Newman, *The early Life of Cardinal Newman*, London, 1891.

Meriol Trevor, *Newman's Journey*, London, 1974.

Maisie Ward, *Young Mr Newman*, London, 1948.

Wilfrid Ward, *The Life of John Henry Cardinal Newman*, 2 vols, London, 1912.

Urban Young, *Life and Letters of the Venerable Father Dominic*, London, 1926.